Original title:
Midnight Verses

Editor: Theodor Taimla
Author: Meelis Maurus
ISBN HARDBACK: 978-9916-763-28-5
ISBN PAPERBACK: 978-9916-763-29-2

Gossamer Gloaming

In twilight's soft and tender glow,
Where whispered winds may lightly show,
A dance of shadows, moonlit grace,
In gossamer, they find their space.

The sky a canvas, hues in blend,
Where night and day in silence end,
Stars awaken, gently bright,
Guiding dreams through velvet night.

Beneath the trees, the secrets keep,
In whispers where the willows weep,
A world unseen, yet ever near,
In glimmers faint, it shall appear.

Through fields of dream and thoughts untold,
A story waits, in threads of gold,
Woven fine by time's own hand,
In gossamer, the tales expand.

Embrace the dusk, let shadows play,
In fragile light, let dreams convey,
Gossamer moments, fleeting, clear,
A whispered world for those who hear.

Twilight Murmurs

Beneath the sky where shadows fall,
Whispers drift through evening's call.
Stars awaken, soft and bright,
Guiding dreams into the night.

Crickets sing in sweet reprise,
Moonlight dances in their eyes.
Every breath, a silent plea,
In the twilight, spirits free.

Leaves caress the whispering breeze,
Gently swaying with such ease.
Moments melt in fading hues,
Eternal echoes to peruse.

Luminous Silence

In the realm where silence gleams,
Light upon our quiet dreams.
Whispers flow in golden streams,
Ebbing thoughts of moonlit beams.

Candles flicker, shadows play,
Night transforms the weary day.
Silent stars align and sway,
Guiding souls along their way.

Eyes closed tight, yet visions clear,
Light and dark, both intertwined dear.
Truths revealed with twilight near,
In luminous silence, none to fear.

Celestial Secrets

Stars above in midnight veil,
Silent secrets they regale.
Constellations' ancient lore,
Whispered through the cosmic shore.

Galaxies in swirling dance,
Tales of wonder and romance.
Light years fade in distant trance,
Embraced by stars' celestial glance.

Mysteries in nebulae,
Unfold with each beseeching sigh.
Infinite the questions why,
In the heavens, answers lie.

Obsidian Dreams

Dark as night in velvet swathe,
Dreams arise from shadows' grave.
Silent pulses, rhythms brave,
In obsidian's embrace they wave.

Echoes of forgotten lore,
Drift through every creaking door.
In the night's eternal core,
Lost in dreams, forevermore.

Blackened skies with hidden gleam,
Silent, dark, as if to scheme.
Every night, a silent theme,
Captured in obsidian dream.

Nightfall Serenade

The sky is dressed in shades of night,
Stars begin their gentle light.
Whispering winds through trees do glide,
Silent shadows softly hide.

Moonbeams dance on lakes serene,
Nature’s nocturne sets the scene.
Crickets sing their lullaby,
Beneath the velvet twilight sky.

In the fields, the fireflies gleam,
Living out their sparkling dream.
Nightfall wraps the world in grace,
A tender touch from time and space.

Hidden Lullabies

In the twilight's soft embrace,
Dreams unfold with gentle pace.
Whispers carried on the breeze,
Secret songs among the trees.

Moonlight bathes the world in white,
Guiding hearts through quiet night.
Stars reveal their ancient tales,
Through the endless cosmic trails.

Listen close, the silence speaks,
Wisdom found in night's mystique.
Hidden lullabies take wing,
In the hush, true peace they bring.

Velvet Nightfall

The evening falls in velvet folds,
Mysteries the night beholds.
Shadows stretch and darken skies,
Softly cloaking weary eyes.

Owls begin their twilight flight,
Guardians of the silent night.
Bats weave patterns through the stars,
Marking time with silent scars.

The world slows in gentle swoon,
Beneath the watchful, distant moon.
Velvet nightfall breathes and sighs,
Wrapping dreams in dark disguise.

Ebon Horizon

As the sun slips out of sight,
Day surrenders to the night.
Ebon horizon stretches wide,
With quiet secrets to confide.

Night anoints the tranquil earth,
Bringing stillness, hinting mirth.
Stars ignite the inky gloom,
Tiny beacons softly bloom.

Mystery in shadows deep,
Nighttime’s promises we keep.
Ebon horizon’s vast expanse,
Capturing hearts in moonlit trance.

Enchanted Eve

The moonlight weaves through ancient trees,
Whispering secrets to the breeze.
Stars align in radiant dance,
On this enchanted eve’s romance.

Fireflies glow in twilight's hue,
A symphony of dreams in view.
Softly spoken words of old,
In silver night, the tale unfolds.

Through the glimmer, shadows play,
Guiding souls who’ve lost their way.
In the night, hearts intertwine,
Bound by whispers, dusk divine.

Hidden Hours

Beneath the veil of silent night,
Mysteries linger out of sight.
In the quiet, hearts reveal,
A thousand secrets they conceal.

Shadows stretch and fade away,
Guardians of the unseen day.
Silent whispers echo near,
Inside the hidden hours, clear.

Moments pass in hushed retreat,
Time suspended, bittersweet.
In the depth of night’s embrace,
Dreams take flight in starlit grace.

Beyond the Eclipse

In a sky of whispered light,
Where shadows cloak the day from sight.
Crowns of darkness softly gleam,
Beyond the veil, a hidden dream.

Stars await the fleeting night,
Glistening through the dimming light.
In the silence, hearts take flight,
Bound by secrets, lost in sight.

In the eclipse, fears alight,
Turning darkness into bright.
Through the dawn, hope persists,
Beyond the shadows, life exists.

Starlit Whispers

In twilight's breath, where stars commence,
Silent whispers leap the fence.
Infinite skies, a canvas vast,
Echoes of the future, past.

Celestial murmurs soft and low,
Guide the dreams that stars bestow.
Across the night, in waves they flow,
Starlit whispers, tender glow.

Through the void, their tales arise,
Connecting hearts across the skies.
In each shimmer, truths unfold,
Starlit whispers, stories told.

Midnight Serenade

The night unveils its soothing veil,
Whispers dance in moonlight's trail,
Stars like diamonds softly glow,
In night's embrace, our spirits flow.

Crickets chime a lilting tune,
Underneath the silver moon,
Shadows weave a tender thread,
As dreams of love and hope are fed.

Trees sway in a gentle breeze,
Speaking secrets to the seas,
Hearts find solace, minds set free,
In this tranquil, midnight spree.

Moonlit Murmurs

Beneath the moon's soft and tender gaze,
Where silvery light casts mystic haze,
Whispers of old, forgotten tales,
Mingle with the midnight gales.

Leaves rustle in silent conversation,
Nature's own sweet incantation,
Nighttime secrets gently shared,
In the moon's glow, hearts laid bare.

Quiet hum of distant streams,
Melds with lovers' whispered dreams,
Moonlit murmurs, soft and light,
Guide our souls through darkest night.

Stargazer's Chronicle

Eyes lifted high to cosmic spans,
Seeking patterns, divine plans,
Constellations, ancient lore,
Light from stars forevermore.

Galaxies whisper tales untold,
In their splendor, fierce and bold,
Mysteries of the universe,
Etched in every twinkling verse.

Voyagers of the night, we soar,
Lost in wonder, evermore,
Map the heavens, find our place,
In the vast, celestial grace.

Dusken Dreams

As sunlight fades to twilight's hue,
The sky displays a purple view,
Birds sing their final, sweet refrain,
Welcoming night's gentle reign.

Soft horizon's lilac sweep,
Lulls the world to tender sleep,
Stars awake in quiet gleam,
Guiding us through dusken dream.

The wind whispers lullabies,
As moonlight kisses teary eyes,
Dreams unfold in night's embrace,
In this magical, tranquil space.

Starlight Sonata

In the quiet of the night,
Whispers of the stars ignite.
Cosmic ballet, soft and bright,
Guiding dreams in silver light.

Twinkling notes, a lullaby,
Celestial chords in velvet sky.
Harmonies that float on high,
Galaxies in hushed reply.

Moonbeams dance on lunar stage,
Ancient tales from page to page.
Echoes from an ageless age,
Crystalline, beyond the sage.

Stardust waltzes, pure and free,
In the cosmic symphony.
Eternal, boundless melody,
Played across infinity.

Astral Reflections

Mirrors of the universe,
Shining through the night's soft curse.
In their light we both immerse,
Cosmic verses, terse yet terse.

Planets spin in silent grace,
Reflecting off your tranquil face.
Astronomical embrace,
In the void's wide-open space.

Constellations forge their ties,
Tapestries that hypnotize.
In their patterns, truths arise,
Secrets locked in ancient skies.

Nebulas with colors swirl,
Brushed with stardust, every pearl.
In this astral, dreamy whirl,
Infinite worlds begin to twirl.

Gloaming Tales

As the sun dips low and fades,
Daylight's fleeting, pastel shades.
Shadows blend in twilight glades,
Nighttime's promise in cascades.

Crickets sing their evening song,
Echoes where the stars belong.
In the dusk, we drift along,
Hours neither short nor long.

Fireflies in fleeting flight,
Glimmer in the waning light.
Softly weaving through the night,
In their glow, the world feels right.

Whispers of the evening breeze,
Rustling through the ancient trees.
Gloaming tales, whispered with ease,
Underneath the sky's deep seas.

Shades of Dusk

As the sun serenely sets,
Dusk reveals its softest nets.
Mysteries in silhouettes,
Painted skies where day forgets.

Purple, pink, and amber hues,
Blend in twilight's tender fuse.
Evening's brush in broad reviews,
Sweeping canvases of blues.

Silent whispers in the air,
Echoes of a world laid bare.
Shades of dusk, beyond compare,
In their beauty, none can spare.

Stars emerge in twilight's glow,
Secrets only dusk can show.
In between the night's slow flow,
Shades of dusk, a twilight bow.

Black Velvet Ode

In shadows deep, where whispers rest,
Black velvet drapes the evening's crest.
Stars concealed in a shroud of might,
A tapestry woven from darkest night.

Serenity folds within its grasp,
Gentle echoes in silent asp.
Dreams emerge, unseen, untold,
On canvas vast, a tale unfolds.

Moonlight's gaze, a fleeting light,
Glimmers softly, faint but bright.
In velvet's hold, the world is stayed,
A silent homage softly paid.

Ebon strands of mystery,
Weaving through our history.
In the night, pure and still,
Black velvet holds an endless thrill.

Ethereal Ebon

In twilight's hush, the ebon mist,
Twines softly like a lover's tryst.
Glimpses of the unknown lie,
Where mortal thoughts dare not to pry.

Whispers float on sable streams,
Fragments of forgotten dreams.
In the hush of shadowed flight,
Truths are hidden from the light.

No dawn's embrace to scatter fears,
Only starlight's silver tears.
In ebon's grace, a world unseen,
A realm of shadows, dark serene.

Beyond the light, beneath the moon,
Lies the ebon's gentle tune.
Singing soft of endless night,
Where darkness reigns in quiet right.

Twilight Hymns

When day and dusk in silence meet,
Twilight hymns in rhythm beat.
Crimson kisses heaven's cheek,
In twilight's arms, all colors speak.

Golden threads of sunlight fade,
Blending where the shadows played.
Night awakens, stretching wide,
As twilight sings, the worlds collide.

Soft and low, the hymn ensues,
Weaving night with varied hues.
Hope and fear in tandem rise,
Mirrored in the twilight skies.

Candles lit on heaven's dome,
As twilight guides the stars back home.
Melodies in shadows blend,
A hymn eternal, without end.

Night's Requiem

In the still of night's embrace,
Whispers weave through endless space.
Stars above, their secrets share,
A symphony beyond compare.

Moonlit paths through dreams we tread,
Guided by the shadows spread.
Echoes from the farthest stars,
Sing of love and ancient wars.

Night's requiem in silence grows,
Mysterious and reposed.
Darkness wraps the world in sound,
In this solitude, we're bound.

As the dawn begins to break,
Night's requiem starts to fade.
Yet its song forever stays,
In our hearts, in endless sway.

Gloom Anthem

Beneath the shroud of endless night,
where silence binds the stars so tight,
a whisper hums through bitter air,
and dreams succumb to dark despair.

The moonlit paths that once were gold,
in shadows lie so damp and cold,
as, cloaked in mist, the hours wane,
the heart laments in quiet pain.

A somber tune the winds are playing,
to secrets lost and hopes decaying,
mournful echoes softly thread,
in this gloaming, fears are said.

Midnight's breath now chills the soul,
and endless blackness takes its toll,
in weary trance, the world does lie,
beneath a sorrow-painted sky.

Whispering Shadows

In twilight's grasp where whispers blend,
a secret path the shadows send,
the ancient trees, with stories fraught,
in midnight's veil are gently caught.

The moonlight spills its silver grace,
on hidden trails the shadows chase,
echoes of the past arise,
through murmured breath and silent sighs.

Beneath the stars, the whispers weave,
the veil of night they softly cleave,
caressing fears with feathered touch,
in realms where shadows speak so much.

A dance of phantoms in the night,
in spectral glow of soft moonlight,
the whispering shadows' silent call,
enchants the stillness, enfolds us all.

Darkened Verse

In realms where light begins to fade,
a darker hymn by night is made,
with ink of stars on velvet sky,
a verse is drawn with shadows nigh.

The echoes of a silent vow,
through twilight's breath, they whisper now,
a tale of sorrow, loss, and woe,
in cadence of the moon's soft glow.

The pages turn in starlit gloom,
unfolding secrets in the room,
where night's own quill inscribes its mark,
in scripts that only shadows hark.

Within this tome of darkened verse,
a universe that does immerse,
the heart in depths of shaded lore,
where dreams and fears entwine once more.

Transient Twilight

Amidst the hues of fading day,
where shadows greet the evening's sway,
the fleeting glow of twilight's kiss,
bemuses hearts with fleeting bliss.

The world transformed in amber light,
between the day and tranquil night,
a transient realm of whispered hue,
where time itself seems ever new.

The stars arise as daylight wanes,
in glistening threads of twilight reins,
while moments fleet and softly fade,
in gentle dance of light and shade.

As twilight melts to night's embrace,
we ponder time's elusive face,
this fleeting hour, so tender, bright,
in transient glow, bids soft goodnight.

Moonlit Echoes

In the hush of a silver night,
Underneath the ancient trees,
Whispers soft in gentle flight,
Carried by the cool night breeze.

Echoes dance on whispering leaves,
Soft as lullabies in air,
Moonlight through the branches weaves,
Painting dreams without a care.

Stars above in silent choir,
Sing of tales beyond our reach,
Hearts are kindled with desire,
Close enough to love, to teach.

Through the silence, songs unfold,
Mysteries the night bestows,
Secrets in the moonlight told,
In these tranquil, moonlit echoes.

Dark Hours Muse

Beneath the shroud of twilight's grace,
Dreams awaken, softly whisper,
In the shadows, find their place,
Darkness makes the muse grow crisper.

Ink and quill in midnight's hand,
Words flow free, unbound by time,
In the quiet, thoughts expand,
Crafting verse and silent rhyme.

Mysteries in night revealed,
Hidden truths in shadows known,
Darkness as a canvas peeled,
Stories on the wind are sown.

In the stillness, muses rise,
From the depths, their voices blend,
In the dark, the spirit flies,
Where creation has no end.

Crescent Shadows

Narrow slice of silver sky,
Crescent moon so shyly hides,
In the night, where secrets lie,
Casting shadows far and wide.

Glimmering with ancient tales,
Silent guardian of the stars,
As the midnight silence hails,
Memories of cosmic scars.

Soft and tender is its glow,
Whispering in twilight’s song,
Hearts are drawn to mysteries, slow,
To the night, where they belong.

Crescent in its arc above,
Shadows weave a moonlit shroud,
Binding hearts with dreams of love,
In the night’s own quiet crowd.

Nocturnal Rhapsody

Symphony of stars alight,
On the velvet sky they sing,
Notes of dreams in pure delight,
Through the night their echoes ring.

Each soft breeze a gentle chord,
Carried through the midnight air,
Nature's voice in calm accord,
Music woven fine and rare.

Crickets play their subtle tune,
Owl's call in rhythmic flow,
Harmony beneath the moon,
Stories on the wind they sow.

In this peaceful, starlit ease,
Hearts will find their nocturne true,
Rhapsody among the trees,
Notes of night-time's sweet renew.

Obsidian Ballet

In darkness steps a silent waltz,
Where shadows bend and night exalts,
Their whispering pirouettes take flight,
Beneath the cloak of endless night.

Ebony slippers tap the ground,
A symphony without a sound,
Ghostly figures twist and spin,
In an obsidian world within.

Midnight's veil drapes the scene,
Glittering stars in serpentine,
Each movement carved in velvet ink,
Dancing on the abyss's brink.

Silent echoes, a dance so rare,
A soul's embrace within the air,
Time dissolves in each ballet,
Obsidian dreams in dark display.

Moonshadow Fantasies

In silver light, the shadows play,
Crafting dreams from night and day,
Whispering tales of long-lost lore,
Moon's allure forevermore.

Shapes that dance upon the walls,
Casting spells in moonlit halls,
Phantoms born from Luna's gleam,
Weave the fabric of a dream.

Beneath a sky of sapphire hue,
Moonshadows bid the night adieu,
Mystic figures softly blend,
Echoes of a world transcend.

Dreams entwined in midnight's veil,
Gossamer threads and silver trails,
Moonshadow fantasies unfold,
In whispered dreams so soft and bold.

Twilight's Lyric

In twilight's hush, the verses bloom,
A serenade to dusk's sweet plume,
Whispers of the day gone by,
Linger in the evening sky.

Gold and violet paint the air,
Twilight's canvas, rich and rare,
Each streak a lyric softly sung,
By the evening's gentle tongue.

Stars awaken, one by one,
Harmonizing with the sun,
The fading light, a tender hymn,
Twilight's lyric, soft and dim.

As shadows lengthen, night descends,
A melody that never ends,
Twilight's song in hues so bright,
Serenades the coming night.

Nebula's Lull

In the cradle of the night,
Nebulas weave their gentle light,
Galaxies drift in silent calm,
Cosmic lullabies and psalms.

Colors swirl in vast expanse,
Stars in cosmic ballet dance,
Each whisper of the stardust true,
Sings a song of born-anew.

Mists of luminescent glow,
Cradle worlds in softest tow,
Nebula's breath, a soothing balm,
In the night's eternal calm.

Slumber deep in cosmic sea,
Dreams of endless infinity,
Nebula's lull, a tender kiss,
In the boundless night's abyss.

Midnight Mirage

In the hush of midnight's breath,
Mirages dance, defying death.
Whispered dreams in shadow's glow,
Secrets only night will know.

Stars align in silent gaze,
Weaving tales of forgotten days.
Through the veil of darkness deep,
Timeless echoes dare to seep.

Moonlight drapes the world in white,
Phantom shapes that haunt the night.
Figures fade and then arise,
Illusions spun beneath the skies.

The desert's chill, the night's embrace,
Mirages flicker, leave no trace.
Ephemeral as a fleeting thought,
By dawn, every dream is caught.

Stardust Chronicles

Journey on through cosmic tides,
Where stardust dreams and secrets hide.
Infinite realms of light and breeze,
Whisper tales among the trees.

Constellations paint the night,
Chronicles in piercing light.
Galaxies of stories old,
In the stars, our fates unfold.

Nebulae with colors bright,
Show us wonders in their flight.
The universe, a sprawling book,
Invites us all to take a look.

Celestial bodies drift in dance,
Each one holds a story's chance.
In the starlit skies above,
We find the truths of endless love.

Lunar Reflections

Beneath the lunar's gentle gleam,
Worlds reflect like silver dreams.
Quiet waters hold the glow,
Of a moonlit, whispered flow.

Shadows form in soft moonlight,
Secrets stirred in the silent night.
Reflections dance upon the shore,
Mysteries that we adore.

Silver rivers weave through air,
Carrying whispers, light as prayer.
Moon's soft glow a tender brush,
Paints the world in silent hush.

In the stillness of the night,
Moon's reflections pure and bright.
Whispered tales in dreams take flight,
Echo through the endless night.

Echoes in the Dark

In the heart of shadows deep,
Whispers in the silence keep.
Echoes from the past arise,
Stories told through midnight skies.

Voices long since spoke, they blend,
In the dark, they never end.
Whispered words of love, of loss,
Echoes softened by time’s gloss.

Night unfolds its velvet wings,
Cloaking us in ancient things.
Memories from forgotten lore,
Echo through, forevermore.

In the quiet, hear them sing,
Tales of shadow, heart, and wing.
As dawn's light begins to mark,
Fade the echoes in the dark.

Evening Epiphanies

Soft twilights drape the day's retreat,
Whispers of stars above collide.
Shadows dance on cobbled streets,
Secrets in night's veil reside.

Moonlight kisses, gentle beams,
Rooftops whisper ancient lore.
Candles flicker, weave their dreams,
Mysteries behind each door.

Cicadas sing melodic tales,
Eclipsing day's chaotic sound.
In twilight's hush, where evening sails,
Serenity and thoughts unbound.

Clouds of amber, skies of ink,
Twilight's cosmic harmony.
Moments still, in thoughts we sink,
Cradled by epiphanies.

Stars emerge, an astral psalm,
Nebulas of dreams ignite.
In evening's fold, we find our calm,
Embraced by soft twilight.

Lunar Laments

Silver tears from lunar eyes,
Glisten on the midnight tide.
Beneath the vast and starlit skies,
Ancient sorrows cannot hide.

The moon, a silent guardian,
Watches o'er the restless sea.
Echoes of forgotten hymns,
Resonate eternally.

Midnight whispers to the breeze,
Carry tales of lost romance.
In the shadows of the trees,
Lonely spirits start to dance.

Through the night, the lanterns glow,
Casting secrets far and near.
In the moon's soft, gentle flow,
Dreams and shadows silently appear.

Awake until the morning breaks,
The moon laments its silent plight.
Within its glow, a heartache wakes,
And fades into the arms of night.

Phoenix of the Night

Flames ignite against the dusk,
Born anew in evening’s light.
From the ashes, gleams of musk,
Rise the Phoenix of the Night.

Wings of fire, soaring high,
Passion reigns where darkness looms.
Stars illuminate the sky,
Embers banish twilight's glooms.

Mystic hues in nocturne's blend,
Velvet skies and spark ignite.
Cycles of an endless end,
Phoenix sings its song of flight.

In each heartbeat, fiery trails,
Burn the shadows into sight.
Through the galaxy it sails,
A beacon in the quiet night.

Rebirth in a fiery sweep,
Dawn will break, the flames succumb.
In the silence, darkness weeps,
Till the Phoenix once again shall come.

Nebula's Embrace

Cosmic tendrils, softly swayed,
Nebula's arms around the night.
Galaxies in colors played,
Weave a tapestry of light.

Stardust whispers, ancient songs,
Painting skies in hues of dreams.
Through the vast, where night belongs,
Glows the universe in beams.

Across the void, the silence speaks,
Nebula's embrace is near.
In its grasp, where wonder peaks,
All our earthly woes appear.

Floating in the astral sea,
Veils of color gently drift.
Moments lost in ecstasy,
Nebula's gift, a cosmic lift.

Boundless realms of starry grace,
Eternal dance in unity.
Cradled in the night's embrace,
A universe of harmony.

Candlelit Confessions

In shadows soft, a secret starts.
Whispers warm, from tender hearts.
Flickers dance, in amber light.
Truths unfold, in quiet night.

Eyes that speak, where tongues do fail.
Souls laid bare, in love's unveil.
Promises, in glow and flame.
Hearts align, and share the same.

Curtains draw, the world outside.
Walls that guard, now set aside.
Hands entwine, in evening's grasp.
Dreams and hopes, two souls clasp.

Candles melt, revealing more.
Locked within, a heart's deep core.
Candor flows, where trust is found.
Love, in whispered words, unbound.

Chasing Stars

Under skies, so vast and wide.
Dreamers lose, their fear and pride.
Stars invite, to worlds unknown.
Cosmos call, where seeds are sown.

Journey starts, with steps so small.
Eyes alight, with dreams that call.
Celestial paths, with light they trace.
Boundless hope, in cosmic chase.

Hearts that beat, in sync with night.
Wings of thought, take flight in light.
Galaxies, where wishes blend.
Horizon meets, where wishes send.

Time stands still, in starlit flight.
Endless realms, of sheer delight.
Infinite, the dreams afar.
Wake each night, to chase a star.

Phantom Pas de Deux

In moonlit halls, where shadows play.
Phantoms dance, the night away.
Whispers soft, in twilight's breath.
Steps that weave, in life and death.

Spectral figures, silent grace.
Ghostly ballerinas trace.
Haunted strains, a soft ballet.
In the night, they find their way.

Ethereal, their movements weave.
Footsteps light, as webs they leave.
Phantom pairs, in silent song.
Through the night, they waltz along.

Glimpses caught, in candle's gleam.
Fading, like a fleeting dream.
Pas de deux, in shadowed glow.
Dance eternal, long ago.

Nocturnal Narratives

When daylight fades, and dusk descends.
Whispers weave, where night extends.
Tales unfold, in quiet dark.
Silent words, that leave their mark.

Midnight winds, their stories share.
Lonely souls, with none to care.
In the hush, of night's embrace.
Mystery, in each shadowed place.

Soft and low, the crickets' song.
Narratives, both short and long.
Under skies, so deep and grand.
Unseen worlds, at our command.

Silent moon, and stars aglow.
Whispered tales, that ebb and flow.
Narratives, of dreams and night.
Written in, the pale moonlight.

Eclipsed Thoughts

In shadows deep where whispers blend,
A mind begins to twist and bend,
Thoughts converge like moon and sun,
In twilight shrouds, they weave as one.

Silent murmurs, silent screams,
Truths beneath the surface gleams,
Moments lost in tangled mesh,
Hearts entwined in midnight's flesh.

Mysteries in corners hide,
Pooling darkness side by side,
Questions drift on silent breeze,
Mind and night in secret ease.

Moon's embrace on restless heads,
Eclipsed dreams on starry beds,
Night unfolds its sable cape,
Veiled thoughts in shadows drape.

Quiet Constellations

Beneath the silent starry light,
Celestial whispers of the night,
Constellations softly gleam,
Reflecting dreams in cosmic stream.

Galaxies on velvet spread,
Whispers linger, words unsaid,
Planets dance in rhythmic ties,
Beckoning with twinkling eyes.

Milky ways in silence flow,
A tranquil symphony below,
Nebulae in colors bloom,
Painting night in quiet plume.

Star by star the night reveals,
Secrets space forever seals,
Constellations mark the trails,
Of whispered tales in cosmic gales.

Through the Veil

Veils of mist in morning's hush,
Nature's whispers in the rush,
Through the veil, the dawn appears,
A tapestry of fleeting years.

Shadows play on waking fields,
Silent secrets night conceals,
Daybreak's light, a gentle hand,
Lifts the veil on timeless land.

Breezes stir the sleeping leaves,
In their wake, the night deceives,
Through the veil, the world reborn,
Morning's kiss on shattered morn.

In the veil, the mysteries keep,
Light and shadow softly weep,
Through the veil we glimpse the true,
Night's retreat and morning's hue.

Night's Ballet

Stars alight on shadowed stage,
As night unveils its storied page,
Cosmic dancers rise and sway,
In night's eternal, silent ballet.

Winds compose a whispered tune,
Guiding steps beneath the moon,
Asteroids in arcs extend,
In graceful twirls, their paths ascend.

Nebulae in colors bright,
Adorn the stage with spectral light,
Silent movements, soft and slow,
In night’s embrace, they ebb and flow.

Galactic waltz in harmony,
Gliding through infinity,
Eclipsed moments softly stray,
In the beauty of night’s ballet.

Lunar Ballad

The moonlight dances on the sea,
Silver whispers in the night,
Stars winking playfully,
In the sky, so vast and bright.

Waves lap gently at the shore,
A lullaby from ocean's deep,
Underneath the moon's allure,
The world begins to softly sleep.

Soft shadows stretch and curl,
Like dreams beneath the azure dome,
In this quiet, peaceful world,
The night is free to roam.

Mysteries in the midnight air,
Secrets told by wind's soft sigh,
Captured in the moon's fair glare,
Till dawn's first light bids them goodbye.

Whispers at Dusk

Twilight settles, calm and still,
Colors blend, the day is done,
Softly, echoes fill the hill,
Whispers of a setting sun.

Shadows lengthen, cool and long,
As stars begin their gentle glow,
The world hums a twilight song,
In a language only night can know.

Trees sway softly to the breeze,
Conversations hushed and low,
As the night takes up the keys,
To unlock dreams and let them flow.

Candles flicker in the dark,
Casting love’s warm tender light,
Guiding hearts like Noah’s ark,
Through the gentle velvet night.

Nocturne's Embrace

Night wraps the earth in shadowed wings,
A blanket soft as velvet's touch,
Where dreams unfold and time just clings,
To moments that don't ask for much.

Stars like sequins dot the sky,
Each a tale from ages past,
Their glow a silent lullaby,
In the void so deep and vast.

Wind whispers its haunting tune,
A melody of ancient lore,
Mixing with the light of moon,
As night unlocks its hidden door.

Peace descends, a gentle grace,
In the arms of night's embrace,
Rest now in this quiet place,
Till dawn's first light begins to trace.

Celestial Reflections

Stars like diamonds, bright and clear,
Mirror worlds beyond our sight,
In their glow, we face our fear,
And find solace in the night.

Galaxies, a distant stream,
Flow across the midnight sky,
Like whispers of a long-lost dream,
Beaconing with a silent sigh.

Planets dance in cosmic ballet,
Orbits intricate and grand,
In the stardust, truths convey,
Knowledge of an endless land.

Hearts reflect in twilight's gaze,
Wandering where heavens blend,
In these countless nights and days,
Eternity finds no end.

Moonshadow Whispers

Beneath the crescent's tender light,
Shadows dance in quiet night,
Secrets shared with breath so slight,
In moonshadow whispers bright.

Stars adorn the sky so high,
Listening as the world lies,
Whispers cross the dreamy sky,
Echoes mingling, yet to die.

Silent lullabies they send,
Through the winds that never bend,
Hearts and wishes they defend,
In moonshadow whispers, friend.

Lonely hours drift to day,
As whispers slowly fade away,
But night returns without delay,
And moonshadow whispers play.

Glimmering with softest grace,
They caress each unseen face,
Leaving not a single trace,
Of moonshadow whispers' embrace.

Starry Eyed Reflections

In the pool of cosmic dreams,
Reflections weave like silver streams,
Starry-eyed, we cast our gleams,
In the boundless space, it seems.

Galaxies in mirrored night,
Whisper tales of ancient light,
Jewels in the deep dark sight,
Guiding us through endless flight.

Constellations draw our gaze,
Echoes of the skies' own maze,
Starry eyes in quiet daze,
Lost within the starlit haze.

We, the children of the stars,
Chart our course without the scars,
In reflections, near and far,
Seeking who we truly are.

Dreams alight in endless skies,
Pull us close to where we rise,
Starry-eyed, we realize,
Reflections hold no more disguise.

Dark Symphony

In shadows' shroud, where silence pulls,
A symphony in darkness trawls,
Notes of sorrow, hope enthralls,
In the night where silence falls.

Whispers weave through hollow air,
Strings of fate in lost despair,
Echoes dance with somber flair,
In the dark's orchestral lair.

Moon's lament, a mournful sigh,
Stars align with night's reply,
Harmony in deep supply,
Where the dark symphonies lie.

Pain and joy in chorded streams,
Play the heart's own silent dreams,
In a weave of seamless themes,
Dark symphony's soft extremes.

Listen close, the night confides,
Secrets sung in echo tides,
Where the dark symphony hides,
In each heart where it abides.

Silhouette Soliloquies

In the twilight's fading crease,
Silhouettes in shadowed peace,
Speak their silent, soft release,
In soliloquies that cease.

Figures cast on wall and floor,
Unseen voices they implore,
Telling tales of sacred lore,
In the night they'll wait no more.

Every move, a whispered grace,
Shadows dance in dark embrace,
Soliloquies in hidden place,
Words unspoken, leave no trace.

Ephemeral in twilight's gleam,
Haunted by a waking dream,
Silhouetted thoughts that team,
Voices blend in seamless stream.

As the dawn begins to rise,
Soliloquies in silence die,
Shadows fade beneath the skies,
Glimmers of their last goodbyes.

Starsong Reflections

Upon the canvas night so deep,
Where stars like whispers softly creep,
A lullaby of distant light,
Guides dreamers through the quiet night.

Moonlit rivers ebb and flow,
Echoes of tales from long ago,
Galaxies dance in silent sway,
As shadows sing till break of day.

Through twinkling veils of cosmic lace,
The universe unfolds its grace,
Star-kissed memories gently drift,
In sleep's embrace, our souls uplift.

Celestial harmonies entwine,
In symphonies of the divine,
Nebulas paint with hues so rare,
Enchantments floating in the air.

Among the stars, reflections gleam,
Whispering secrets in a dream,
Eternity in moments brief,
Starsong's tender, sweet relief.

Astral Veil

Through the astral veil we peer,
Beyond the bounds of atmosphere,
Where mysteries of time and space,
Unfold within a starry embrace.

Planets orbit in their trance,
Eternal in their cosmic dance,
Whispers of the void resound,
In the silence, truth is found.

Nebulas like dreams unfurl,
In the realms of the astral swirl,
Distant whispers call our names,
From stars alight with ancient flames.

Galactic tides shift and flow,
Cosmic currents ebb and grow,
In the darkness, beauty's framed,
Celestial wonders, untamed.

Through the veil our spirits soar,
Beyond what we have known before,
In the astral's boundless sea,
We glimpse the depths of eternity.

Silence of the Stars

In the silence of the stars,
Where the universe sheds its scars,
A tranquil void where dreams reside,
Across the night vast and wide.

Constellations whisper low,
Secrets only night can know,
In their stillness, we find grace,
Eternal peace in endless space.

Planets spin in quiet might,
Through the velvet cloak of night,
Celestial bodies drift in tune,
Beneath the watchful, ancient moon.

Nebulas in silence bloom,
Ghostly flowers in the gloom,
Silent echoes, time's caress,
In cosmic calm, we find our rest.

Amid the stars' unspoken hymn,
Our souls find solace, gentle and dim,
In their quiet, timeless art,
Resides the stillness of our heart.

Dreamer's Enclave

In the dreamer's enclave bright,
Where reveries take their flight,
Stars whisper secrets of the night,
Guiding us with gentle light.

Nebulous dreams cascade and fall,
In this haven, we heed the call,
Of possibilities untold,
In cosmic arms, we are enfold.

Galactic mists and stellar streams,
Weave the fabric of our dreams,
Each star a beacon, glimmering,
In the night they softly sing.

Through the realms of sleep we stray,
In the dreamscape's vast array,
Infinite realms we explore,
Where fantasy and starlight soar.

In this sanctuary so divine,
Every dream is a sign,
Of a journey yet to start,
In the heart of every star.

Veiled Melodies

Beneath the sky where secrets sleep,
In whispered winds, the echoes deep,
A song of old through trees doth sweep,
In veiled melodies, hearts weep.

Mountains hum a distant tune,
Rivers laugh beneath the moon,
Nature's choir, the spirits swoon,
In veiled melodies, dreams commune.

Oceans murmur tales of yore,
From ancient depths to whispering shore,
Ethereal notes, forgotten lore,
In veiled melodies, souls explore.

Stars reveal a symphony,
In night's embrace, such harmony,
Celestial chords, infinity,
In veiled melodies, eternity.

So listen close when darkness falls,
And hear the past in hidden calls,
For in the night, the mystic sprawls,
In veiled melodies, the world enthralls.

Nightfall Symphony

As twilight tints the sky with gold,
The night’s orchestra takes its hold,
In whispered notes and stories told,
A symphony of dreams unfold.

Whispers wind through leaves so grand,
Under stars’ soft, guiding hand,
In this glowing, tranquil land,
Nightfall's music—elegant, planned.

Crickets join with lullabies,
Owls' songs and fireflies,
Together weave the night's reprise,
Within the symphony, hearts rise.

Moonlight dances on the lake,
Ripples form, and shadows wake,
In the calm, the notes partake,
Nightfall's symphony doth quake.

In the stillness, close your eyes,
Feel the music's gentle ties,
Let your spirit realize,
Nightfall's symphony, the heart complies.

Silent Starfall

In the quiet, calm of night,
Twinkling gems of purest light,
Silent starfall out of sight,
Whispers secrets, soft and bright.

Glistening in the velvet sky,
Falling stars with silent sigh,
Painting dreams as they pass by,
In the silence, wishes fly.

Ephemeral, their silvery streaks,
Silent beauty that each seeks,
Upon the night's calm, gentle peaks,
Where the heart in silence speaks.

Each star’s fall a silent plea,
Of cosmic dreams and mystery,
Sailing through infinity,
In the silent starfall sea.

Close your eyes and make a wish,
In the night’s sky, silent swish,
For in the quiet, purest bliss,
Silent starfall grants its kiss.

Moon's Monologue

Upon the stage of twilight blue,
The moon begins its tale anew,
A monologue both old and true,
Of dreams that night and stars ensue.

Glimmering on night's painted stage,
Reflecting tales from age to age,
With wisdom penned in every page,
Moon’s soft monologue doth engage.

Casting light on lovers' sighs,
And tears beneath the shadowed skies,
In every beam, a thousand eyes,
Moon's monologue, where mystery lies.

Through clouds it sails, a ghostly guide,
Unveiling truths the dark would hide,
In its glow, dreams coincide,
Moon's monologue, a gentle tide.

So listen close and hear its voice,
In moonlit hush, hearts rejoice,
For in its tale, we find our choice,
Moon's monologue, our inner noise.

The Witching Hour

When midnight chimes, the air is still,
A shadow dances on the hill,
Whispers float on breezes thin,
As moonlit secrets now begin.

Candles flicker, casting light,
On ancient tomes of mystic might,
The cauldron bubbles, voices hum,
For now, the witch's time has come.

Stars align, a silver glow,
Enchants the world we think we know,
Figures cloaked in velvet night,
Challenge fate within their sight.

Mysteries hidden in the dark,
Reveal their truths with just a spark,
For in the hour 'twixt day and night,
Magic reigns in purest light.

Spells are woven, dreams ignite,
Unseen forces join the fight,
As shadows deepen, grow, and tower,
Bow to none, The Witching Hour.

Ebon Echoes

In the vale where shadows sleep,
Secrets in the darkness seep,
Ebon echoes loud and clear,
Whisper tales of yesteryear.

Night's embrace, a velvet shroud,
Silence speaks in voices loud,
Ancient oaths and long-lost lore,
Resonate forever more.

Midnight winds through forest sway,
Memories in moonlight play,
Every rustle, each faint cry,
Echoes of a time gone by.

Mysterious murmurs fill the air,
Remnants of a mystic prayer,
Ebon echoes, soft and true,
Call to those who dare pursue.

In the dark where dreams conspire,
Find the past in whispered choir,
Bound by night, the secrets grow,
Ebon echoes, we now know.

Dusk's Embrace

When the sky in twilight flames,
Glimmering gold, the horizon tames,
Day retreats in amber hues,
As nightly dreams begin their cues.

Whispered winds in fading light,
Guide the way to coming night,
Shadows lengthen, colors blend,
Marking where the shadows bend.

Soft, the world slips into calm,
Night, a sweet and cooling balm,
Stars appear in gentle grace,
Within the arms of dusk’s embrace.

Hushed serenades of evening’s breath,
Sing of both life and quiet death,
Beneath the twilight’s gentle pull,
Nighttime’s cloak becomes so full.

In these moments, soft and sweet,
Day and night in silence meet,
Harmony in twilight’s face,
We find peace in dusk’s embrace.

Night's Serenade

When day departs and sun withdraws,
Night emerges without pause,
Soft sonata, stars align,
Begins the nocturne, so divine.

Owls call in moonlit glades,
Breezes play in twilight shades,
Crickets join with rhythmic cheer,
Music only dark can hear.

Mystic tunes on silver streams,
Flow beneath the land of dreams,
Every note, a secret played,
Composes night’s serenade.

Quiet vibes in shadow’s tune,
Harmonize with rising moon,
Each soft whisper, each small sound,
A symphony in dark profound.

When night's curtain softly sways,
And stars illuminate their rays,
Listen close as dreams invade,
To the calm of night's serenade.

Gilded Shadows

Golden whispers brush the leaves,
Sunlit shades in twilight's weave,
Quiet secrets, night receives,
Dreams that shadows softly cleave.

Dappled gold on ancient bark,
Silent echoes, moonlit arc,
Hidden in the evening's dark,
Light and shadow, never stark.

Beneath the canopy of night,
Glimmers dance, a fleeting sight,
Lost within the dusky light,
Shadows gilded, yet so slight.

Whispered winds through twilight trees,
Golden shadows on the breeze,
Mysteries that none can seize,
In the dark, yet hearts at ease.

Gilded shadows fade away,
Merging with the break of day,
In the twilight, they shall stay,
Till the night reclaims its sway.

Darkened Radiance

Velvet skies in moon's embrace,
Stars enshroud the night's cool face,
Softly glowing, lost in space,
Darkened radiance, time's trace.

Silver beams across the sea,
Shadows cast by ancient tree,
Mystic light sets spirits free,
In night's darkened mystery.

Celestial paths, a starlit song,
Lonely lights where dreams belong,
In the vast, forgotten throng,
Darkness brightens, pure and strong.

Ebon curtains gently fall,
Mists arise as nightbirds call,
Radiant dark, the empty hall,
Midnight's whispers, one and all.

Silent echoes in the deep,
Memories in shadows keep,
Darkened radiance as we sleep,
In twilight's hold, our hearts to steep.

Silhouettes in Starlight

On the canvas of the night,
Figures dance in silver light,
Silhouettes in starlit flight,
Echoes of a world so bright.

Underneath the cosmic dome,
Shadows find a fleeting home,
In the starlight, spirits roam,
Boundless, free to softly comb.

Lunar beams cast shadows tall,
Mystic figures, silent call,
In the dark where dreams befall,
Silhouettes enchant us all.

Galaxies in distant play,
Silhouettes in soft array,
In the night, they gently sway,
Guiding us, the stars' own lay.

Etched in light against the black,
Figures trace a gentle track,
In starlight's embrace we lack,
Nothing but the night's calm back.

Moonsong Nocturne

Underneath the moon's soft gaze,
Silver songs in evening's haze,
Notes of night in mystic phase,
Moonsong whispers through the maze.

In the quiet nocturne's hold,
Melodies of ages old,
Secrets in the starlight told,
Lunar tales in whispers bold.

Harmonies in twilight air,
Gentle tunes without a care,
Moonsong lifting hearts that dare,
Dreams that in the night repair.

Ethereal the nightbird's tune,
Singing to the patient moon,
Moonsong weaving soon to soon,
In the darkened, calm commune.

In the silence, moonsong plays,
Guiding through the night's long days,
Nocturne's gentle, soothing lays,
In the moon's eternal rays.

Ethereal Nocturne

The moonlight drapes a silken veil,
Whispering secrets, ancient tales.
Stars align in cosmic grace,
Time dissolves without a trace.

Night's embrace, a phantom dance,
Dreams cascade with every glance.
Soft winds hum a lullaby,
Mysteries of the sky.

Silent echoes, shadows blend,
Infinite realms where thoughts transcend.
Celestial rapture, midnight’s bloom,
In the quiet, hearts resume.

Ethereal beings flutter near,
Speaking truths through the atmosphere.
Enchanted world of silver light,
Guiding souls through endless night.

Sacred whispers, boundless theme,
Lost within a lucid dream.
Eclipsing dawn with twilight’s tune,
In this ethereal nocturne.

Shadows at Zenith

At the zenith, shadows grow,
Merging with the ebb and flow.
Whispered secrets from the night,
Casting spells in fading light.

Dancing forms with silent grace,
Unseen spirits fill the space.
Veiled in mystic, dark disguise,
Hidden truths beneath disguise.

Chasing echoes of the past,
In twilight's grip, they hold me fast.
Phantoms of forgotten lore,
Wander through the evermore.

Night’s enigma, veiled and stark,
Guides me through the endless dark.
In the vortex, time stands still,
As shadows bend to twilight’s will.

Midnight whispers, soft and low,
Lost within the twilight's glow.
Bound by secrets, hushed and deep,
In shadows at zenith, I’ll keep.

Starlit Serenade

Beneath the vault of endless sky,
Soft melodies begin to fly.
Starlit whispers, sweet ballet,
Orchestrates the night's display.

Harmony of silent dreams,
Flows through twilight's silver streams.
Cosmic symphony unfurl,
Woven in the astral swirl.

Stars like diamonds, gleam and glow,
Eternal songs they softly show.
Infinite, this grand parade,
In the starlit serenade.

Silver notes and melodies,
Lift the heart and bend the knees.
Cosmic rhythm, hushed and pure,
In the night's embrace, secure.

Celestial choir, soft and free,
Sings a song for you and me.
Night's enchantment, softly played,
In this starlit serenade.

The Witching Song

In the twilight's eerie call,
Phantom whispers softly fall.
Magic stirs, the night grows strong,
Echoes of the witching song.

Charming words, with ancient might,
Spiral in the dead of night.
Mystic, dark, and wild dream,
Holds us in a spectral beam.

Samhain's breath, the night unveils,
Ancient lore, the moon exalts.
Vervain, rosemary entwined,
Hexes of another kind.

Candles flicker with a sight,
Shadows twist within their light.
Rituals of old evoke,
Memories of spells bespoke.

Enchantress, with her voice so clear,
Sings the song we all revere.
Boundless magic, dark yet strong,
In the thrall of the witching song.

Celestial Candles

In the velvet sky they glow,
Glitters of the cosmos sway.
Candles of the night bestow,
Light that guides our dreams' way.

Stars ignite the boundless sea,
Waves of light in dark's embrace.
Hopes and wishes, wild and free,
Etched in this celestial place.

Silent murmurs, endless shine,
Whispers from a higher sphere.
Infinite, their grand design,
Echoes through the night's veneer.

Galaxies of ancient lore,
Beacons of the heavens tall.
Timeless dance forevermore,
Celestial candles call.

Dreamers gaze with hopeful hearts,
Into the vast and starry lanes.
Witness how the magic starts,
When the universe refrains.

Nocturne's Whisper

Shadows fall, the world sleeps still,
Nighttime's hush, the air does chill.
Softly speaks the evening's spell,
In the dark, where secrets dwell.

Moonlight casts a silver cloak,
On the trees, with quiet stroke.
Stars commence their silent song,
In the sky where they belong.

Winds do sigh with breath unseen,
Through the leaves a soft routine.
Gentle whispers, night's delight,
In the arms of quiet night.

Dreams arise with twilight's gleam,
Floating on a starry stream.
Murky thoughts like shadows creep,
Underneath where memories sleep.

Nocturne's whisper, sweet and deep,
Carries tales and souls to keep.
In the night, our hearts confide,
Whispered secrets far and wide.

After Dusk

Golden sun dips out of sight,
Leaving trails of amber light.
Dusk departs, the night arrives,
Nature's rhythm, dark connives.

After dusk, where shadows play,
Dreams unfold in quiet sway.
Hushed the world, in moon's soft glow,
Secrets through the night do flow.

Crickets sing their lullaby,
Underneath the starlit sky.
Whispers on the cool night's breeze,
Swaying gently through the trees.

Night holds tales of long ago,
Beneath its cloak, they softly flow.
Waking dreams and silent sighs,
Blinking with each star that lies.

After dusk, the world transforms,
Into realms where magic forms.
Silent shadows, moonlit lands,
Nighttime takes us by the hands.

Twilight's Soliloquy

As the daytime starts to fade,
In the twilight's quiet shade.
Whispers of the night begin,
Softly as the dusk sets in.

Colors blend in sky's embrace,
Pastel hues in woven lace.
Stars emerge, their voices keen,
In the twilight's in-between.

Soft the air with evening's breath,
Echoes of the day's bequeath.
Twilight speaks in whispers low,
Tales of yore in moonlit glow.

In this hush, the heart does see,
Night's own soliloquy.
Dreams and visions softly kissed,
In the velvet evening mist.

Twilight's charm, a seamless seam,
Weaves together night and dream.
Lullabies in shadows sing,
On night's stage, the stars do cling.

Eclipsing Hour

In the stillness of the night,
The moon began to fade,
Stars whispered their light,
As shadows softly played.

Time seemed to gently freeze,
Beneath the veiled sky,
The world in hushed appease,
As day and night did vie.

The silence broke a tale,
Of dreams so sweetly spun,
Eclipsing details frail,
Till dawn erased the sun.

Nocturnal Whispers

The night breaths soft and low,
With whispers through the trees,
A gentle, fleeting show,
Of secrets in the breeze.

Stars adorn the vast above,
Their silent stories told,
A canopy of love,
In silvern, radiant fold.

Creatures of the night do sing,
Their melodies so pure,
Beneath the moonlight's wing,
Eternal dreams ensure.

Haunting Twilight

As the sun began to wane,
Twilight softly crept,
Over land, sea, and plain,
Until the shadows wept.

Whispers of the past emerged,
In the dimming glow,
Memories unanointed surged,
From ages long ago.

A haunting echoed sweet,
From corners dark and deep,
In twilight's soft retreat,
Old secrets scorned by sleep.

Shadowfall Lyrics

Shadows fall in dusky veil,
Binding day with night,
Where whispers of the moon prevail,
In soft, enfolding light.

Through the silent corridors,
Of stars and dreams they tread,
Exploring cosmic shores,
In realms where suns have fled.

Words unsaid and songs unvoiced,
In dark they find their place,
Shadowfall, where hearts rejoiced,
In the night’s tender embrace.

Dusky Prelude

The sky's a kiss of twilight hue,
In whispers soft, the night comes through.
A serenade of silent streams,
The dusk unfurls its velvet dreams.

Beneath the stars, in muted gold,
The evening’s secrets yet untold.
A gentle breeze begins to sing,
In dusky prelude, hearts take wing.

The trees are cloaked in mystery,
Their shadows writhe in harmony.
A world between the day and night,
In twilight’s arms, our souls take flight.

The twilight spreads its ancient lore,
A bridge to worlds unknown before.
Between the light and dark we dance,
In dusky prelude’s mystic trance.

The hush of night begins its reign,
With promises of dreams arcane.
Embrace the dusk, where magic lies,
In silent prelude, under skies.

In Shadow’s Hold

The moonlight casts a silver glance,
The darkness leads a ghostly dance.
In whispers low, the secrets told,
Embrace of night, in shadow’s hold.

The stars like sentinels do shine,
Guardians of the night's design.
Their watchful eyes in blackened skies,
In shadow’s hold, the mystery lies.

The owl’s soft hoot, the cricket’s song,
In shadow’s hold, where nights belong.
A realm where dreams and fears unfold,
In silent whispers, truth is told.

A world of night where shadows blend,
And all the boundaries start to bend.
In darkness deep, we search and mold,
Our deepest fears, in shadow’s hold.

So journey forth through shadow's sway,
Where night dissolves into the day.
In shadow’s hold, our spirits fly,
Beneath the ever-watchful sky.

Dreamer’s Dusk

The sun descends, a slow retreat,
With twilight dreams at dusk we meet.
A pastel world begins to spin,
In dreamer’s dusk, the night begins.

Horizon blushes soft in hue,
A tranquil scene, a sky anew.
In dreamer’s dusk, our minds take flight,
To realms of wonder, out of sight.

The city lights, they start to gleam,
Awakening the nighttime dream.
A tapestry of soft delight,
In dreamer’s dusk, the lull of night.

The world is hushed, a gentle pause,
As shadows dance without a cause.
In dreamer’s dusk, let's drift away,
To lands unseen at close of day.

With stars above, the dreamer's guide,
We sail through nights in quiet stride.
In dreamer’s dusk, the magic flows,
And in the dark, our spirits glow.

Veiled Harmonies

The night descends, a veil of sound,
In whispered tones, the dusk is crowned.
With harmonies of stars and skies,
In veiled symphony, the magic lies.

The crickets chirp, their song begins,
A melody where twilight spins.
In veiled harmonies of night,
Each note a journey, pure delight.

The rustling leaves, the night owl's call,
Blend into symphony of all.
In veiled harmonies, we find,
A peace that soothes the wandering mind.

The nightingale sings soft and low,
In moonlit glow, the rivers flow.
In veiled harmonies, we tread,
Where every note and dream is led.

So let the night's sweet music play,
In veiled harmonies, we lay.
Entranced by dark's enraptured theme,
In silent chords, we weave our dream.

Nightshade Poetics

In shadows deep where nightshade dwells,
A whisper soft, a silent spell,
The moonlight weaves its silver threads,
Amidst the stars, a violets' bed.

The twilight sings a sombre tune,
Beneath the gaze of pallid moon,
Where shadows dance in muted grace,
A fleeting dream, a hidden face.

The nightshade blooms in quiet night,
Its petals shed in phantom light,
A tale unfolds, serene and dark,
Lit by the ghostly fireflies' spark.

In hushed embrace, the twilight sighs,
As echoes blend with softened cries,
Beneath this veil, where secrets lie,
The nightshade whispers a gentle goodbye.

Amidst the silence, shadows play,
In nightshade poetics, dreams waylay,
Yet in the morn, as daybreak nears,
Its tender verses disappear.

Ephemeral Light

In breaking dawn, a transient gleam,
Of gold that glosses every dream,
A fleeting wisp of morning dew,
That fades before it paints the view.

The sunlight dances on the wave,
Each radiant bead, a moment saved,
Yet as they sparkle, shadows chase,
Ephemeral light, a brief embrace.

A whispering wind through budding leaves,
A sunlight touch, a heart that believes,
These ephemeral kisses of the sun,
In fading vistas, each day begun.

The tales of light in fleeting hue,
A canvas painted, always new,
Though shadows come to steal its breath,
It lives in us, beyond its death.

Thus in each dawn, resplendent grace,
In ephemeral light, we find our place,
In moments short, yet ever bright,
We cherish the ephemeri of light.

With every turn, the light renews,
A timeless dance with countless views,
Ephemeral yet lasting long,
Within our hearts its radiant song.

Cosmos of Night

Upon the canvas of the sky,
The stars like scattered dreams pass by,
In endless stretch, the night unfolds,
A tapestry of myths retold.

The cosmos sings in silent shroud,
Each twinkling star a note, unbowed,
A symphony of distant gleams,
In depths of space, a sea of dreams.

Bathed in the light of spectral beams,
The universe, a place that teems,
With galaxies and worlds unseen,
In cosmos vast, our thoughts convene.

Amidst the dark, the constellations gleam,
The night a stage for cosmic scheme,
The dance of stars, celestial flight,
Unfolds the secrets of the night.

Each stellar point a sun so bright,
In distant realms, it shares its light,
We gaze in awe, in silent prayer,
To the cosmos of night, beyond compare.

The galaxies in swirling grace,
Reflect the endless, boundless space,
In cosmos of night, our dreams find flight,
Eclipsed in wonder, lost in night.

Gloaming Whispers

In twilight's hush, the world grows still,
Soft whispers float on evening's chill,
Shadows stretch, begin to dance,
In the gloaming's gentle trance.

Fireflies flicker in the fading light,
Stars begin their silent flight,
The day sighs its final song,
In the gloaming, we belong.

Leaves rustle and softly sway,
As night replaces the fleeting day,
Moonlight glows in water's shimmer,
Gloaming whispers grow dimmer.

Through the dusky veil we gaze,
Eyes alight with twilight's haze,
On the edge of night’s tender seam,
We whisper secrets, we drift, we dream.

Candlelit Dreams

In a room with shadows tall,
Candlelight begins to sprawl,
Flickering flames in silent streams,
We are lost in candlelit dreams.

Warmth that glows, a tender kiss,
Moments captured in soft bliss,
Whispered words in the amber light,
Candlelit dreams take flight.

On the walls, our stories play,
Dancing lights, they guide the way,
In this tender, fleeting gleam,
We find solace, we dare to dream.

Fading wax, the hour grows late,
In this glow, we contemplate,
Between the shadows and the beams,
We are bound by candlelit dreams.

Nocturnal Epiphanies

Under the veil of midnight's cloak,
Epiphanies in whispers spoke,
Stars align in cosmic grace,
Nocturnal thoughts take their place.

In the quiet hours of night,
Dreams and visions come to light,
Whispers of the stars above,
Nocturnal epiphanies, we love.

Moonlight casts its silver gleam,
Overlaying life's swift stream,
In the stillness of night’s embrace,
We find truth, we trace the grace.

Through the darkness, minds unfurl,
Mysteries of the midnight whirl,
Epiphanies in silent screams,
Awakened by nocturnal dreams.

Celestial Melancholy

Beneath the stars, a somber sigh,
Tears that gleam in the night sky,
Celestial tales in whispers told,
Melancholy in the cold.

Night's embrace, a quiet grief,
In the cosmos, find relief,
Starry skies of endless blue,
Carry sorrows, old and new.

Constellations weave a tune,
Songs of sorrow softly croon,
In the celestial vast expanse,
Melancholy in a trance.

Through the cosmos, hearts will yearn,
For love lost and to return,
In the silence of the night,
We find comfort in starlight.

Milton Keynes UK
Ingram Content Group UK Ltd.
UKHW021946280724
446162UK00003B/42

9 789916 763285